POND CARE

John Dawes

HAMLYN

Published 1986 by Hamlyn Publishing,
Bridge House, London Road, Twickenham, Middlesex

ISBN 0 600 30730 1
Printed in Italy

Some of the illustrations in this book are reproduced from other books published by The Hamlyn Publishing Group Ltd

Contents

Introduction 4

Which Type of Pond 5

What Materials to Use 6

Choosing the Site 8

Designing the Pond 11

Pond Construction and Installation 12

Fish 20

Plants 24

Looking After Your Pond 28

Index 32

Introduction

A well-managed pond is a beautiful, relaxing, worthwhile addition to any patio or garden. A badly managed one can end up as a water-filled, smelly, green hole in the ground.

Given the choice, it seems reasonable to conclude that no-one would dream of opting for the latter. Yet, some people do precisely this, simply by ignoring the basic rules of pond care. These rules are both logical and easy to follow. All the major ones are described in this guide in the hope that they will help you establish and maintain an attractive pond, full of healthy fish and plants for you to enjoy.

Small, typical liner pond, with lilies planted in baskets in the deeper part and marginals on the shallow shelves.

Which Type of Pond

A little time spent choosing the most appropriate type of pond will pay rich dividends later on. The most popular types and their characteristics are as follows:

Informal Pond Irregular shape (lack of obvious symmetry). Relatively wide selection of plants and/or fish.

Wildlife Pond Irregular shape. Selection of plants and fish restricted to native species. All forms of natural waterlife encouraged – including frogs, toads, newts, and dragonflies.

Formal Pond Artificial shape, with symmetrical matching sides common. Even if the patterns are not repeated, the pond outline shows obvious signs of planning. Range of plants and fish usually more restricted than in informal set-ups. Ornaments, fountains and cascades are common features.

Tub/Sink Pond Small water features with restricted stocks of plants and fish. Ideally suited for small areas.

Clearly, it is important to match a particular type of pond to the surrounding layout. For instance, a wildlife or informal pond will look quite out of place in a strictly formal garden or patio set-up. The opposite is, of course, equally true.

What Materials to Use

Irrespective of which type of system you decide upon, you will have a range of possible materials to choose from. Each has a number of advantages and disadvantages and these should be weighed up carefully before a final decision is taken.

Concrete, Cement, Bricks and Blocks

Advantages Extremely durable; wide range of designs possible from completely informal to formal; ideal for raised, formal layouts.

Disadvantages These materials are not easy to work with unless one is familiar with their properties and the relevant techniques; not ideally suited for use during hot, dry weather or if frosts are a possibility; repairs are difficult to effect; contains highly toxic lime – decontamination/sealing essential.

Liners

Advantages Can be used virtually throughout the year; easy to use.

Polythene: inexpensive; flexible.

PVC: strong, flexible and stretchable.

Butyl: very durable; flexible and stretchable.

Disadvantages Need to be hidden from view by plants, rockwork, etc; wrinkles are difficult to avoid.

Polythene: not very durable; sensitive to ultra-violet radiation; non stretchable.

PVC: not cheap. Not as durable as butyl and, therefore, not ideal for truly permanent features.

Butyl: expensive.

Prefabricated

Advantages Pre-determined shape and simple installation. Very good for quarantine/treatment purposes, rearing of fry, tadpoles, etc. Safe for children to use. Light to handle and available in formal and informal designs.
Plastic: very light and inexpensive.
Glassfibre: durable, reasonably priced.
Black polyester: very strong and durable; wider range of deeper designs than with plastic and glassfibre.
Disadvantages Pond may be small and/or shallow and, therefore, not well-suited to winter survival; predetermined shape provides little flexibility.
Plastic: not very durable.
Glassfibre: relatively few models are more than 45 cm (18 in) deep (some deep ponds of this type do exist though).
Black polyester: more expensive than plastic and glassfibre.

Two-level brick pond built on a foundation slab and painted inside to waterproof it.

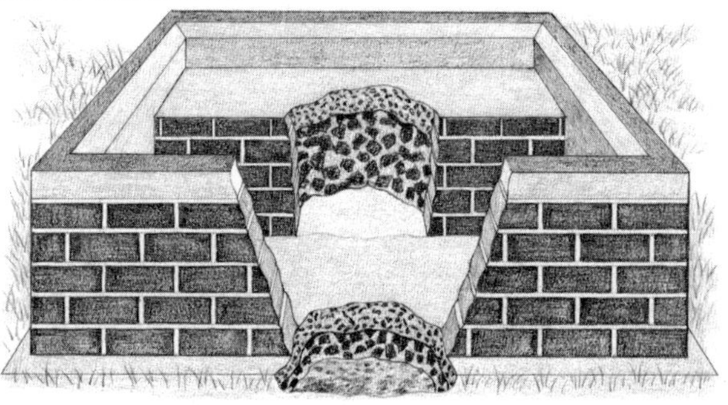

Choosing the Site

As with the other factors mentioned so far, time should be set aside when choosing the best site for a pond. The following points are the most significant ones when considering a suitable location:

Open locations Receive high levels of illumination and warm up quickly – good for plant growth and health of fish. Algal problems that may arise because of high illumination can be controlled. Open sites are relatively free of leaf-fall and root damage problems. Mid-day protection from sun is desirable but not essential.

Flat or gently sloping terrain Looks more natural than steeply sloping locations. Relatively easy to landscape and/or arrange to provide all-round viewing of the pond. Makes all parts of the pond accessible. Reduces risk of rocks and soil rolling down into the pond.

Low-lying sites above water table These are the most natural-looking sites for informal and wildlife ponds.

Sites offering protection from prevailing winds Tender young plant growth is protected during early stages. Tall, fully-grown/pot-bound plants will not topple over.

Sites within easy reach of electricity Helps with installation of fountains, pumps, filters, lights and other electrically-driven accessories.

Sites close to and viewable from within the house Provide

Position the pond carefully: this one avoids overhanging trees and shadows from the house.

interesting, different aspects of the pond and allow viewing at all times. Facilitate control of certain predators, such as cats and herons.

North-facing sites Receive lower levels of light and lower temperatures than other aspects, particularly if close to a wall or building.

Sites close to trees If site is too near trees, root damage to the pond can occur. Minimum recommended distance: equal to eventual height of tree. Some species have poisonous leaves and/or seeds. Leaf-fall can also cause pollution, especially when pond ices over. Others can act as overwintering sites for certain pests.

Steeply sloping terrain Soil and rocks will roll down into the pond unless they can effectively be prevented. Landscaping and construction can prove very difficult.

Cold spots or frost hollows Experience lower temperatures than most other sites, with the possible exception of north-facing locations.

Wet spots – below existing water table Difficult to work in. Unsuitable for setting concrete. Liners can be pushed up by water pressure from below. Prone to flooding during wet weather.

Raised site Informal ponds can look unnatural on raised sites unless landscaping, perhaps using soil excavated during construction, can be used to create the illusion of 'lowering' the pond.

Designing the Pond

There is no such thing as the perfect pond that will meet everyone's requirements and expectations, as well as catering for all the needs of fish and plants. Even so, it is possible to make some general recommendations which are well worth bearing in mind when designing a pond. It may prove impossible to follow every one to the letter, but the closer one can get to them the better.

1) A pond should have the highest volume to surface area ratio possible for its size, ie the deeper for a given size, the better. This will minimize fluctuations and help provide a stable environment.

2) A pond should have the largest surface area possible within the limits imposed by the site. This should not be less than 4.5 sq m (50 sq ft).

3) The shape of a pond should be pleasant, but simple and open to avoid localized trouble spots and facilitate maintenance.

4) A pond profile should be as steep as possible (but not vertical), except in wildlife schemes (saucer-shaped). A slope of 1 in 3 should be aimed for.

5) One level of 30 cm (12 in) wide marginal shelving should be provided at a water depth of 22 cm (9 in).

6) The depth of a pond should not be less than 45 cm (18 in). A depth of 60 cm (24 in) would be preferable.

Pond Construction and Installation

Although a pond can be installed at any time of the year, not every month is perfectly suitable for every kind of pond.

For example, irrespective of the type of materials being used, extremely cold climatic conditions must be avoided. There are several reasons for this: some materials become difficult to work with at low temperatures; another factor is that digging a hole in frozen ground, even if it were possible, is best left to martyrs. Why break your back in order to dig a pond when just a little patience will make the job both easier and more enjoyable?

There are, of course, other considerations. Liners, for

Estimating the size of a liner.

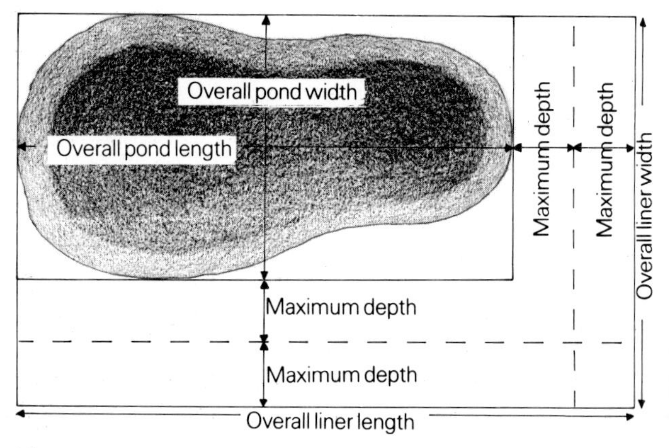

instance, become rather inflexible during cold weather and may require 'softening' in a warm room prior to use. Working with concrete under severe climatic conditions can prove extremely difficult. For a start, hard frosts will prevent concrete from drying out properly and, although the addition of a special 'anti-freeze' can help, this is best left to the professionals. At the other extreme, very hot, dry weather can accelerate the drying process to such an extent that cracks may form. This, naturally, dictates against late spring and summer as being appropriate for concrete pond building. If no alternative is available, then wet sacking spread out over newly-laid cement will slow down the drying process and will help reduce the risk of cracks developing.

Installation techniques

Lined ponds Pond liners normally come complete with directions on how to install them. Nevertheless, a brief discussion outlining the main points of selection and installation may prove helpful.

It is, obviously, very important to estimate the size of liner accurately. This can be done quite simply:
(a) Measure the maximum length of the pond. (b) Measure the maximum depth of the pond. (c) Multiply the figure obtained for the depth by 2. (d) Add this figure to the length obtained in (a). *This will give you the length of liner required.* (e) Measure the maximum width of the pond. (f) Add the figure obtained in (c) (depth × 2) to the width. *This will give you the width of liner required.*

Note PVC and butyl are both flexible and stretchable. The figures obtained above will, therefore, provide

sufficient liner to fit the hole and leave enough surplus for trimming round the edges. Polythene is not stretchable. Therefore, to ensure that you have enough material for tucking in under edging slabs, etc, allow 30 to 60 cm (1–2 ft) extra all-round.

The theory of pond excavation is, without doubt, easier than the practice! Nevertheless, the job has to be done. Here are the main steps (which may need modifying according to circumstances):

(a) Remove obstructions from pond site.
(b) Excavate the pond outline.
(c) Excavate the rim ledges.
(d) Dig down to shelf level.
(e) Remove stones and other sharp objects.
(f) Continue digging down to ultimate pond depth, plus 5 cm (2 in).
(g) Repeat (e).
(h) Prepare excavation to receive liner, using sand or other suitable cushioning materials, eg polythene bags, newspapers, felt, and foam.

Prefabricated Ponds These ponds can be installed either raised, with a supporting wall, or sunken, ie at ground level. The former involves a more complicated approach and is out of the scope of this guide. The directions which follow are, therefore, concerned solely with sunken schemes (although they can be adapted with some ingenuity to apply to raised ponds as well):

(a) Mark out a rectangular shape large enough to encompass the whole pond.
(b) Excavate a hole 22 cm (9 in) larger than the rectangle and 5 cm (2 in) deeper than the pond.

(c) Clear the excavation of sharp stones and compact the base.
(d) Cover the bottom with cushioning material (see Lined Ponds).
(e) Fit pond into excavation, support the shelves, check that everything is level and that the pond rim is slightly below surrounding terrain (the pond will rise slightly as a result of (f)).
(f) Backfill the space with compacted soil.

Concrete Ponds Concrete ponds, like prefabricated ones, can be either raised or sunken. Only sunken ones are dealt with here (for the same reasons given for raised prefabricated ponds). The directions given apply to a small-to-medium-sized informal pond:

Side view of lining for concrete pond.

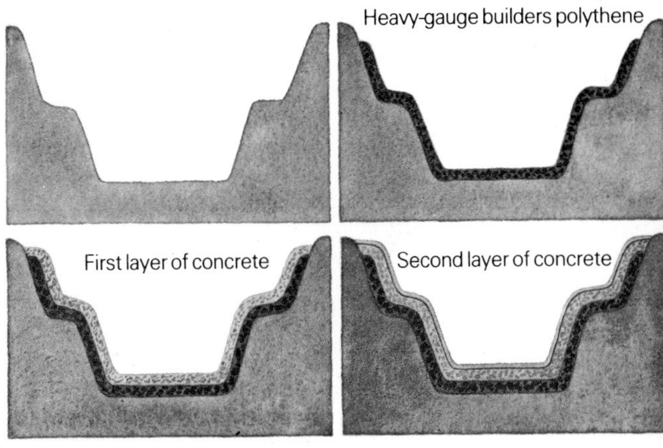

(a) Excavate pond following general principles described for lined ponds but make allowances for: 15 cm (6 in) hardcore; 15 cm (6 in) base; and 10 cm (4 in) sloping sides.
(b) Lay compacted hardcore to depth of 15 cm (6 in).
(c) Prepare and mix concrete (3 parts coarse aggregate; 2 parts sharp sand; 1 part cement).
(d) Lay bottom and sides to depth of 12 cm (5 in).
(e) Allow concrete to set overnight.
(f) Prepare cement mixture (3 parts sharp sand; 1 part cement) – add waterproofing or colouring powder if required.
(g) Add smooth 2.5-cm (1-in) layer of cement (rendering) to base and sides.
(h) Allow cement to dry, covering with damp sacking if necessary.

Making a liner pond: (A) pool shape marked out and levelled off; (B) hole lined with sand; (C) filling with water; (D) trimming excess liner.

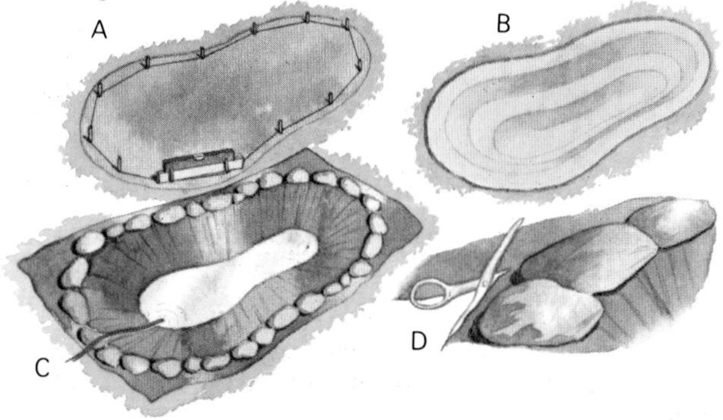

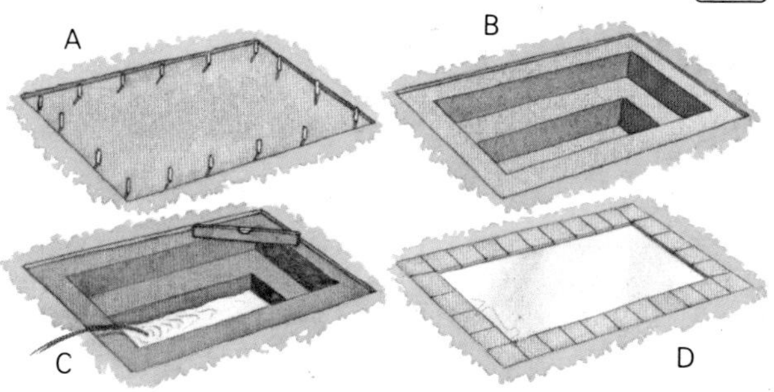

Prefabricated pond: (A) hole dug to shape; (B) prefabricated liner in position; (C) filling with water; (D) finished pond.

(i) Fill pond with water (anytime between 1–7 days after (g)).
(j) Drain pond after one day and allow to dry out completely if sealing is desired. (Sealing compounds are available from several manufacturers and carry full instructions.) Otherwise, refill pond and commence maturing process by periodic filling, draining and refilling.

Note: large ponds, both of informal and formal types, require a reinforcing mesh embedded in the cement. Formal ponds additionally involve the use of wooden shuttering. Both these techniques require detailed treatment that only larger reference books can provide.
Tub and sink ponds Tub ponds are now regularly available through water garden centres or other aquatic outlets, while sink ponds generally have to be put together using a ceramic kitchen sink covered in a cement/peat mixture.

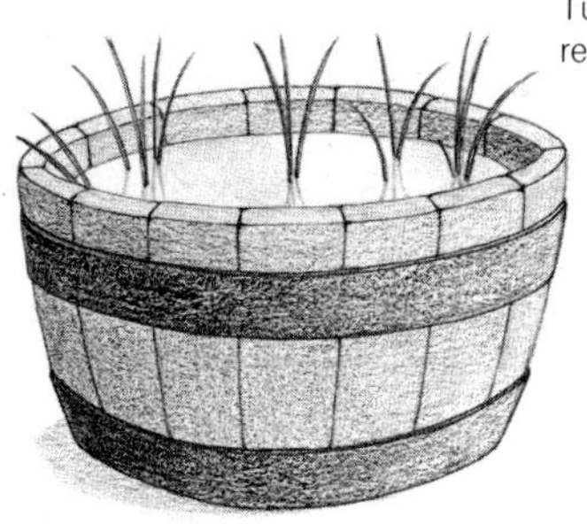

Tub ponds are ideal for restricted spaces.

The small size of both these types of pond makes them ideal for restricted spaces and can provide attractive, colourful displays during the pond season. On the debit side, these small containers can only hold a restricted range and quantity of plants and/or fish. In addition, tub and sink ponds are unsuitable as overwintering quarters for the vast majority of fish and quite a few plants.

Moving water The inclusion of a pump in the overall plans for a pond opens up a host of possibilities – filtration, improved aeration, fountains, waterfalls, watercourses and cascades.

Personal tastes and finances will, of course, both play major parts in the final choice. Even so, several criteria should be borne in mind, irrespective of this:

1 Pump output and pond size should be closely matched. A small pond fitted with a powerful pump is far from ideal – so is a narrow pond with a wide-spraying fountain.

2 Watercourses, waterfalls and cascades look best when used on their own, *not* in conjunction with a fountain.

3 Fountains look out of place in a wildlife water scheme but are impressive, and compatible with, formal systems.

Advice on all these factors should be sought from specialist dealers, some of whom have working displays to help you make your final decision. Any method that results in disruption of the water surface will help aerate the water and allow toxic carbon dioxide to escape. Fountains, waterfalls, courses and cascades all fall into this category. It is, therefore, important to make allowances for the installation of at least one of these features. Even if finances are restricted, there should be something to meet your needs.

The same applies to filters which not only remove dirt from the water but can also purify it by neutralizing toxic waste products such as ammonia and nitrites. Again, advice on what best meets your needs and circumstances is available from all dealers.

Fountains make attractive features and help aerate the water.

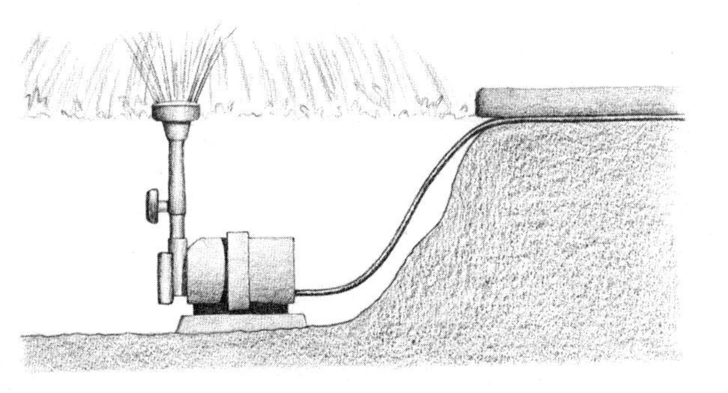

Fish

Selection of fish for the pond

Goldfish (*Carassius auratus*). Available in many forms. The short-finned and slim-bodied varieties are the strongest – Common Goldfish, Shubunkins, Comets and Fantails.

Koi (*Cyprinus carpio*). These fish grow very large and therefore require deep ponds. Full-scaled varieties are stronger than the 'naked' (fewer scales) ones.

Orfe (*Leuciscus idus*). Gold-coloured fast-swimming fish that are best kept in shoals.

Koi

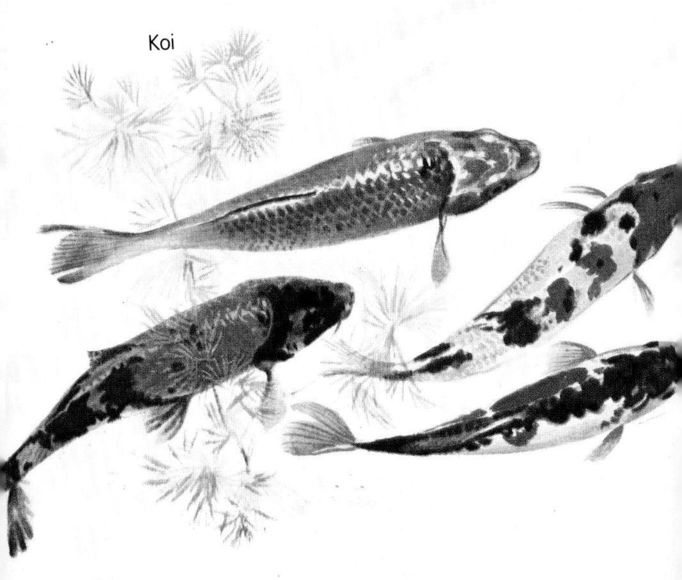

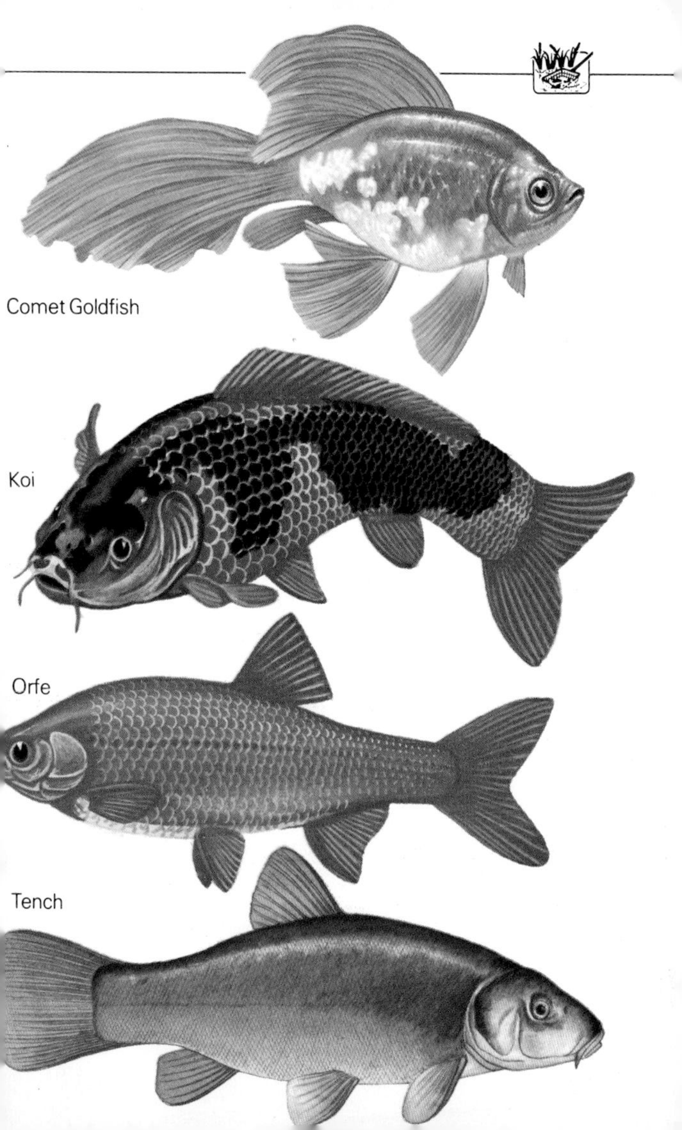
Comet Goldfish
Koi
Orfe
Tench

Tench (*Tinca tinca*). Bottom feeder available in green and golden forms.
Rudd (*Scardinus erythropthalmus*). Golden form now available. Looks best as a shoal.

Fish stocking levels It is important to accept from the start that we cannot cheat nature – a certain amount of water can only accommodate a certain number of fish. Aeration and filtration both help to increase the 'carrying capacity', but only within limits. A safe stocking level is to allow 150 sq cm (24 sq in) of pond surface for every 2.5 cm (1 in) of fish, excluding the tail.
Buying fish Some good pointers to watch out for in a healthy fish are: erect fins (except in some long-finned varieties); lively disposition; balanced swimming; full body; good appetite; intact fins (no tears); no missing scales; no injuries, lumps or sores. If you buy a fish with these characteristics, the chances are that it is healthy. Some internal diseases are not detectable in their early phases, so you can never be 100 per cent certain of a fish's state of health.
Quarantine Many aquatic shops sell fully quarantined stocks. If they are not, the first batch can be kept in a trough (or the pond itself) for up to two weeks before any other fish are introduced, just to make sure that everything is all right. Should treatment be necessary this should be carried out elsewhere. This should be done with all subsequent fish introduced.
Introducing fish Carrying fish home in a newspaper-wrapped polythene bag or insulated polystyrene box will give them some protection and help them settle down. Having got them home, the following steps

should be carried out in full:
(a) Float the bag in the pond for about 15 minutes or so (up to one hour if the volume of water is large) to allow the temperature of the bag water gradually to reach that of the pond.
(b) Untie the bag – *do not burst it* – and mix in a small amount of pond water (ending up with a mixture of approximately 1 part pond water to 3 parts bag water).
(c) Leave the bag in the pond for a further 10 minutes or so, resting the open end on the pond surround and weighing it down with a rock.
(d) Repeat steps (b) and (c) at least once more. This allows the fish to get used to their new water chemistry in several small stages.
(e) Gently tip out the fish into the pond – avoid 'pouring' them in.

Fish health Many of the fish diseases are difficult to diagnose and/or treat and are, therefore, best left to specialists – the experienced fish keeper or vet. Of those that are easily diagnosed, the most common are:
White Spot: seen as pin-sized spots on the body and fins.
Fungus: appears as whitish, fluffy (cottonwool-like) patches on the fins and body.
Flukes: flicking against objects is a good sign to look for.
Fin and Body Rot: tattered, blood-shot fins and ulcers.

In addition: ulcers, loss of colour or condition, raised scales, blood spots, and others, are all indicative of bacterial infections and require antibiotic treatment (see vet for prescription). In general, most diseases are kept at bay by good water quality and a balanced maintenance routine. (See *Hamlyn Pet Guides: Fish Diseases and Treatments* for more information.)

Plants

Selection of plants for the pond

Submerged oxygenating plants Canadian Pondweed (*Elodea canandensis*), 'Crispa' (*Lagarosiphon major*), Hornwort (*Ceratophyllum demersum*), Milfoil (*Myriophyllum*), Curly Pondweed (*Potamogeton crispus*).

Floating plants Fairy Moss (*Azolla caroliniana*), Water Soldier (*Stratioites aloides*), and Frogbit (*Hydrocharis morsus ranae*). In summer, Water Hyacinth (*Eichhornia crassipes*) and Water Chestnut (*Trapa*) are also available.

Surface plants Water lilies – very wide selection available. Check on final maximum size before you buy. In addition, try Water Hawthorn (*Aponogeton distachyus*), Water Fringe (*Nymphoides peltata*) and Golden Club (*Orontium aquaticum*).

Marginal plants Some species growing well in most soil or shallow water: Iris (numerous types to choose from), Sweet Flag (*Acorus*), Water Plantain (*Alisma plantago-aquatica*), Bog Arum (*Calla palustris*), Marsh Marigold/King Cup (*Caltha palustris*), Cotton Grass (*Eriophorum*), Manna Grass (*Glyceria*), Lobelia (*Lobelia cardinalis*), Monkey Flower (*Mimulus*), Water Forget-me-Not (*Myosotis palustris*).

Deeper water plants Flowering Rush (*Butomus umbellatus*), Umbrella Grass (*Cyperus*), Pickerel Weed (*Pontederia cordata*), Arrowhead (*Sagittaria*), Zebra Rush (*Scirpus tabernaemontanii zebrinus*), Dwarf Reedmace/

Group of plants from each section of the pond: deep water, marginal, floating and submerged oxygenating plants.

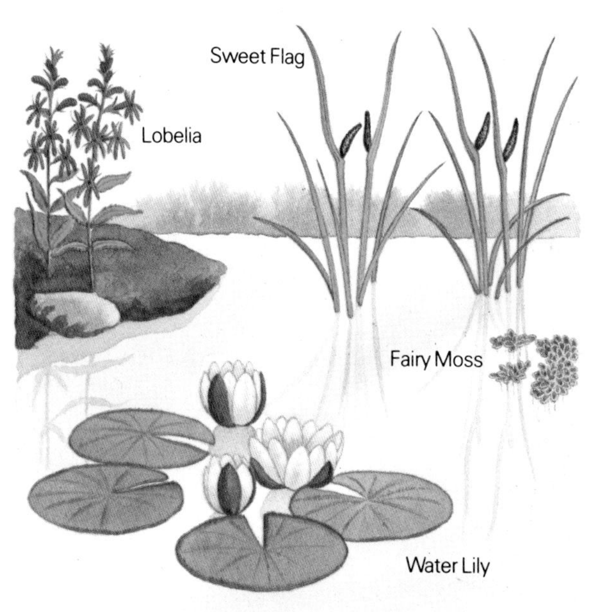
Sweet Flag
Lobelia
Fairy Moss
Water Lily

Canadian Pondweed

Dwarf Bulrush (*Typha minima*), and Arum Lily (*Zantedeschia aethiopica*).

Plant stocking levels Plants carry out a process known as photosynthesis during daylight hours. This involves the absorption of carbon dioxide to produce carbohydrates. All organisms require carbohydrates (humans included) but only photosynthetic organisms can build them up from their basic components. Plants are, therefore, vital as the first step in the provision of carbohydrates. Some animals will eat the plants directly, while others will eat the animals that eat the plants . . . and so on.

A further contribution made by plants is that they actually generate oxygen as one of the by-products of photosynthesis. Again, all organisms, including the plants themselves, require oxygen. During the day, plants generally produce more oxygen through photosynthesis than they require for respiration, thus helping to aerate the water. However, when daylight fades, photosynthesis stops (it is dependent on light). Respiration, of course, carries on.

Submerged oxygenating plants In addition to generating oxygen, these plants absorb chemicals through their leaves and roots. Fortunately, some of these chemicals are precisely those required by algae. Therefore, a good stock of submerged oxygenating plants will help keep a pond clear.

Floating plants These have floating leaves and roots suspended in mid-water. Besides the obvious attractions of certain species, all are useful in ponds as a means of surface cover. Some species, such as Duckweed (*Lemna*), can undergo population explosions which can prove difficult to control.

Surface plants These have floating leaves and anchored roots. The best-known and most spectacular examples are provided by Water Lilies.

Marginal plants Usually referred to simply as Marginals, these plants have roots anchored either underwater or in moist soil, and aerial leaves.

Planting techniques Submerged oxygenating plants can either be weighted down in bunches and dropped into the pond or, preferably, bedded into a seed tray or other suitable container filled with sand, gravel or soil.

Surface and marginal plants should be planted either in proper baskets or perforated pots. If a plant basket is used, this needs to be lined with hessian or liberally perforated polythene as a first step to prevent the rooting medium from slipping out.

This is followed by a layer of stones to help stabilize the container and a firm layer of rooting medium such as turf, garden soil or loam. Special fertilizer blocks are widely available and one of these can be added at this stage. A final layer of gravel on top of the planting medium will protect it from the attentions of fish and will, therefore, help to keep water turbidity down. The crowns of surface plants must project slightly above the level of the rooting medium (they may rot otherwise). Once planting has been completed, the containers must be lowered *gently* into position. If they are plunged into the pond, much of the painstaking work done beforehand will be destroyed.

Looking After Your Pond

A new pond takes time to mature fully, the process starting literally from the moment water is introduced. The art of pond care lies in maintaining all parameters within tolerable limits, keeping major fluctuations under control at all times and providing both fish and plants with everything they need.

Food, oxygen and favourable environmental con-

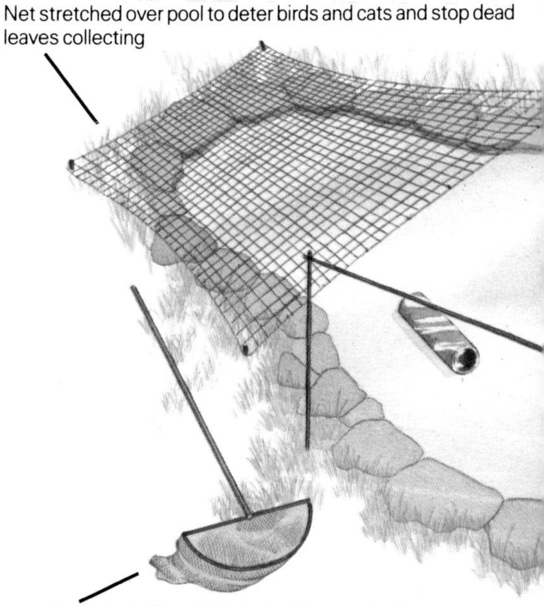

ditions are perhaps the three main factors contributing to success or failure. Oxygenation and environmental control are dealt with elsewhere (see page 18). From the feeding point of view, there are two main factors that can cause problems: choosing the right food; and feeding the correct amounts. Choosing adequate food is easy as a visit to any shop or centre will show. If you need any advice, a word or two with a member of staff will soon put you right.

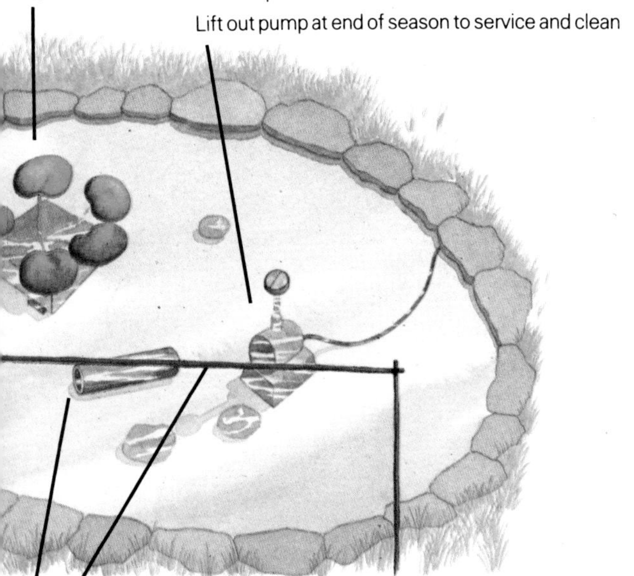

As far as the quantity of food is concerned, the 'five-minute rule' should ensure that overfeeding is avoided. According to this rule, the correct amount of food is that which will be completely consumed *within five minutes.* During the growing season, five or six such feeds per day may be necessary. Between late autumn and early spring, however, demand for food will disappear completely and no food should, therefore, be given once the temperature of the water drops below 40°F (4.5°C).

Year-round Pond Care

Spring Fish are sluggish and plant growth is limited during early spring (Marsh Marigolds are an exception). Feed fish very sparingly and only when they show signs of active searching. Carry out a partial water change (running a hose into the pond for several hours will do the trick). Use dechlorinator and water conditioner. Feed fish regularly from mid-spring onwards. If water turns green, *do not* carry out a second water change. As plant growth improves, green water should disappear. The process can be speeded up through the use of algicides. Fish will begin to spawn in spring. Late spring is a good time for planting or for a general clean-out of an established pond.

Summer Pests, such as Dragonfly nymphs and Water Boatmen, may become abundant. Usually, they do little damage. Diving Beetles pose a more serious threat. Constant removal with a hand net should keep things under control. Many pondkeepers do not consider most visitors as pests, excluding Diving Beetles or excessive infestations of Dragonfly nymphs.

Plant pests, such as some midges and beetles, may

cause damage to leaves. If infestation is severe, remove affected leaves or submerge affected plant for several days. Extreme cases should receive a gentle dose of insecticide – take the plants away from the pond.

Plant and fish growth are at their most vigorous. Feed fish very regularly – on demand if necessary. Spawning activity will continue through summer. Regular 'hoovering' of pond bottom will prove helpful during the summer months.

Autumn Fish will feed well into autumn as long as temperatures do not drop excessively. If cold weather sets in, reduce feeding – cease feeding altogether towards the end of autumn. Protect pond from leaf fall by covering with a net. Alternatively, remove leaves several times each day. Cut back submerged oxygenating plants, remove dead leaves and blooms from surface plants and tidy up marginals. Carry out a partial water change as in spring.

Winter No feeding should be carried out. Thin ice will generally thaw out daily. Thick ice will prevent escape of toxic gases which can kill off fish. Keep a hole open at all times by using a pond heater, or by thawing out a new hole each day with hot water, either poured directly on to the ice or indirectly by pouring it into a container, like a can. 'Squeezable' objects – ballasted polystyrene boxes or plastic bottles – can also be used. Balls, as long as they are not too light, can be floated on the surface and will help to keep small areas ice-free.

On no account must a hammer or other heavy object be used to create a hole. This practice is cruel, potentially dangerous, unnecessary and inexcusably unfair on the fish.

Index

Page numbers in *italic* refer to the illustrations

aerating water 19, 22, 26
algae 8, 26
algicides 30
ammonia 19

baskets, plant 27
blocks 6
body rot 23
brick ponds 6, *7*
butyl liners 13–14
buying fish 22

cement ponds 6, 13
choosing sites 8–10, *9–10*
cold spots 10
cold weather 12–13
comet goldfish *21*
concrete ponds 6, 13, 15–17, *15, 16*
construction and installation 12–19

dechlorination 30
deep water plants 24–6, *24*
depths, water 11
designing ponds 11
diseases, fish 22, 23

electricity 9
excavating ponds 14

feeding fish 28–30, 31
filters 19, 22
fin rot 23
fish
  buying 22
  diseases 23
  feeding 28–30, 31
  introducing to pond 22–3
  species 20–2, *20, 21*
  stocking levels 22
flat locations 8
floating plants 24, 26–7, *24*
flukes 23
formal ponds 5, 17
fountains 18–19, *19*
frost 10, 13
fungus diseases 23

goldfish 20, *21*

hot weather 13

ice 31
informal ponds 5, 9, 10
insecticides 31
installation 12–19

koi 20, *21*

leaf-fall 8, 10, 31
liners *4*, 6, 12–14, *12, 16*
locations 8–10, *9–10*
low-lying sites 9

marginal plants 24, *24*, 27
materials 6–7
mesh, reinforcing 17
moving water 18–19

nitrites 19
north-facing sites 10

open locations 8
orfe 20, *21*
oxygenating plants 24, *24*, 26, 27, 31
oxygenation 28–9

pests 10, 30–1
photosynthesis 26
plants 24–7, *24, 25*
  pests 30–1
poisonous leaves 10
polythene liners 14
ponds
  choosing sites 8–10, *9–10*
  construction and installation 12–19
  designing 11
  introducing fish to 22–3
  looking after 28–31
  materials 6–7
  plants 24–7, *24, 25*
  types 5
prefabricated ponds 7, 14–15, *17*
profiles, ponds 11
pumps 18
PVC liners 13–14

quarantine, fish 22

raised ponds 14, 15
raised sites 10
reinforcing mesh 17
root damage 8, 10
rudd 22

shapes, ponds 11
shubunkin *20*
shuttering 17
sink ponds 5, 17–18
sites, choosing 8–10, *9–10*
sloping locations 8, 10
sunken ponds 14–15
surface area 11
surface plants 24, 27

tench *21*, 22
trees
  leaf-fall 10, 31
  root damage 10
tub ponds 5, 17–18, *18*

water
  aerating 19, 22, 26
  changing 30, 31
  filters 19, 22
  freezing 31
  moving 18–19
water table 9, 10
wet spots 10
White Spot 23
wildlife ponds 5, 9, 11
winds, protection from 9
wooden shuttering 17